Andrew Brodie Basics

LET'S DO TIMES TABLES

FOR AGES 5-6

with over **100** reward stickers

- Over 300 practice questions
- Regular progress tests
- Thorough tables practice

Published 2015 by Bloomsbury Publishing Plc
50 Bedford Square, London, WC1B 3DP

www.bloomsbury.com

ISBN 978-14729-1662-4

Copyright © 2015 Bloomsbury Publishing
Text copyright © 2015 Andrew Brodie
Cover and inside illustrations of Ollie the Owl and Andrew Brodie © 2015 Nikalas Catlow
Other inside illustrations © 2015 Judy Brown (Beehive Illustrations)

A CIP catalogue for this book is available from the British Library.

10 9 8 7 6 5 4 3 2 1

Printed in China by Leo Paper Products

This book is produced using paper that is made from wood grown in managed, sustainable forests. It is natural, renewable and recyclable. The logging and manufacturing processes conform to the environmental regulations of the country of origin.

To see our full range of titles visit **www.bloomsbury.com**

BLOOMSBURY

Notes for parents

What's in this book

This is the first in an exciting new series of *Andrew Brodie Basics: Let's Do Times Tables*. Each book contains more than 300 multiplication table questions, especially devised to cover the key requirements of the National Curriculum.

At the early part of Key Stage 1, pupils will be taught to use multiplication facts from the two, five and ten times tables. They will probably be provided with equipment such as counters, toy cars, toy bears, etc so that they can see the mathematical processes in action e.g. they may be asked to 'find three sets of two bears' or to 'count out four sets of five cars'. They may also be encouraged to draw or colour in pictures showing items arranged in twos, fives or tens and they may be shown items arranged in 'arrays' e.g. this array might be used to show two sets of five or five sets of two:

○ ○ ○ ○ ○
○ ○ ○ ○ ○

How you can help

To get the most out of this book, find time to sit with your child while they work through the activities and discuss the questions with them, explaining any terms they are not familiar with. To begin with, your child may find the activities and progress tests quite tricky and they might get quite a few questions wrong. Make sure that they don't feel disheartened by this. Instead, give your child lots of praise and explain that everyone makes mistakes and that's how we all learn!

The level of difficulty increases gradually throughout the book but some questions are deliberately repeated. This is to ensure that children have the opportunity to revisit vital new facts – they may not know the answer to a particular question the first time they encounter it but with another opportunity later on children are given a second chance. Don't be surprised if they need to practise certain questions lots of times!

You might find it helpful to put up posters on the bedroom wall, showing multiplication facts for the two times, five times and ten times tables. Talk about these facts with your child.

Ollie the Owl

Ollie the Owl sits at the top of the page and is full of wise comments to help your child through the learning process!

Brodie's Brain Boosters

Brodie's Brain Boosters feature short mathematical problems which can be solved by working logically. Some of these may look very straightforward but the thinking processes that your child will need to

apply are important skills to practise, ready for more challenging work later on. Understanding the wording of questions is a crucial aspect of problem solving so ensure that your child reads each question carefully – help them with the vocabulary if necessary.

With lots of practice your child will see their marks improve day by day. By the end of the book you should be able to see a real improvement in their maths and hopefully a positive attitude too!

Lots of things come in twos. I've got two eyes.

1 set of 2 eyes

1 x 2 = 2

2 sets of 2 eyes,
so 4 eyes altogether

2 + 2 = 4
2 x 2 = 4

3 sets of 2 eyes,
so 6 eyes altogether

2 + 2 + 2 = 6
3 x 2 =

4 sets of 2 eyes,

so ⬚ eyes altogether

2 + 2 + 2 + 2 =
4 x 2 =

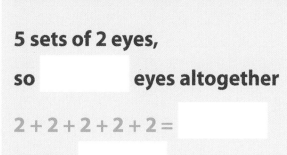

5 sets of 2 eyes,

so ⬚ eyes altogether

2 + 2 + 2 + 2 + 2 =
5 x 2 =

Complete the first part of the two times table.

one two is two	➡	1 x 2 = 2
two twos are four	➡	2 x 2 = 4
three twos are six	➡	3 x 2 =
four twos are eight	➡	
five twos are ten	➡	

3

Learning the two times table

Look at this array of circles. Ring the circles in sets of two. The first two have been done for you.

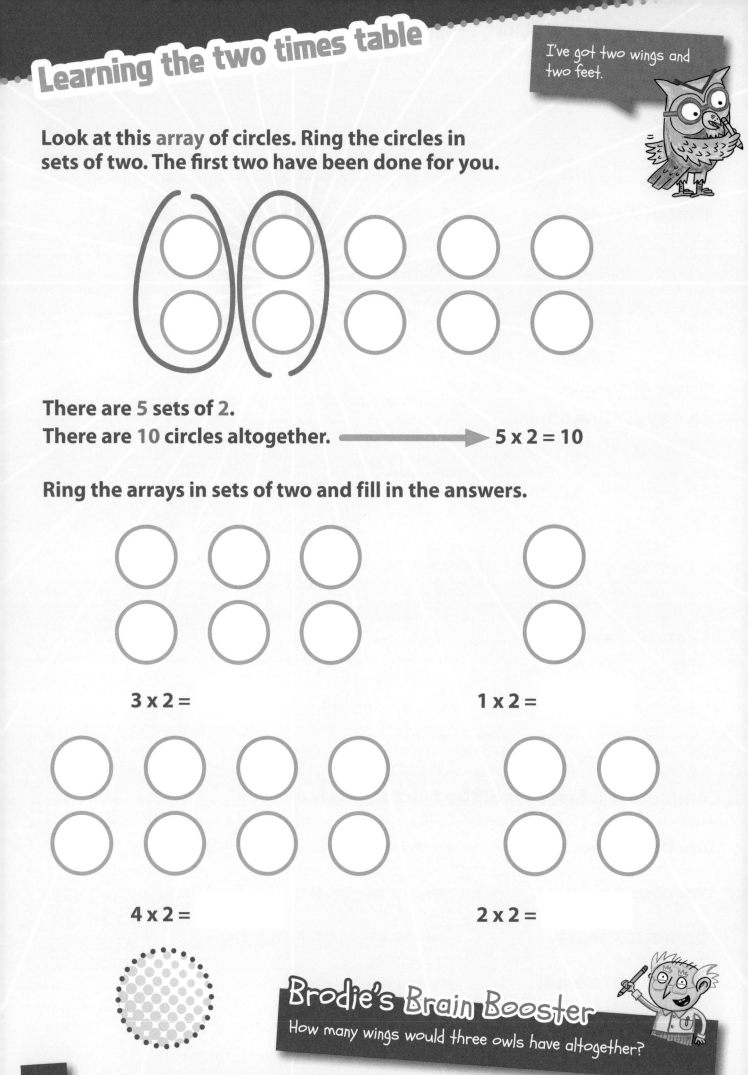

There are **5** sets of **2**.
There are **10** circles altogether. ➡ **5 x 2 = 10**

Ring the arrays in sets of two and fill in the answers.

3 x 2 =

1 x 2 =

4 x 2 =

2 x 2 =

Brodie's Brain Booster
How many wings would three owls have altogether?

4

I've got two feet but I don't need socks!

**Sort the socks into pairs by joining them with a line.
The first pair has been done for you.**

Complete the first part of the two times table.

one two is two	➝	1 x 2 = 2
two twos are four	➝	2 x 2 =
three twos are six	➝	
four twos are eight	➝	
five twos are ten	➝	

**All the answers to the two times tables questions are even numbers.
Colour the even numbers.**

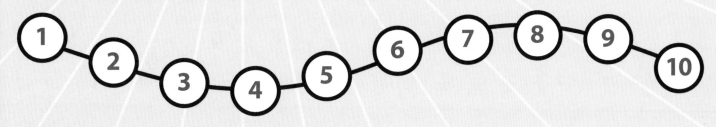

Which numbers did you colour?

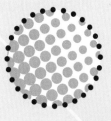

Six twos

I've got two feet but I don't need boots!

How many **pairs** of boots can you see?

How many boots **altogether**?

$6 \times 2 =$

Match the boots in pairs of two.
The first pair has been done for you.

$6 \times 2 =$

one two is two	→	$1 \times 2 = 2$
two twos are four	→	$2 \times 2 = 4$
three twos are six	→	
four twos are eight	→	
five twos are ten	→	
six twos are twelve	→	

Colour the even numbers in blue.

Which numbers did you colour?

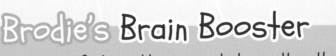

Brodie's Brain Booster
How many feet would seven owls have altogether?

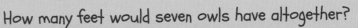

Seven twos

I've got two eggs in my nest.

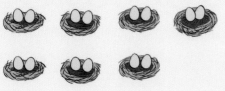

How many nests can you see?

How many eggs can you see?

7 x 2 =

Look at this array of eggs. Ring the eggs in sets of two.

7 x 2 =

one two is two	⟶	1 x 2 = 2
two twos are four	⟶	2 x 2 = 4
three twos are six	⟶	
four twos are eight	⟶	
five twos are ten	⟶	
six twos are twelve	⟶	
seven twos are fourteen	⟶	

Colour the even numbers in red.

1　2　3　4　5　6　7　8　9　10　11　12　13　14

Which numbers did you colour?

1 Write the missing numbers.

1 3 5 7 9 11 13

2 Ring the stars in twos.

4 x 2 =

3 Match the socks in pairs.

7 x 2 =

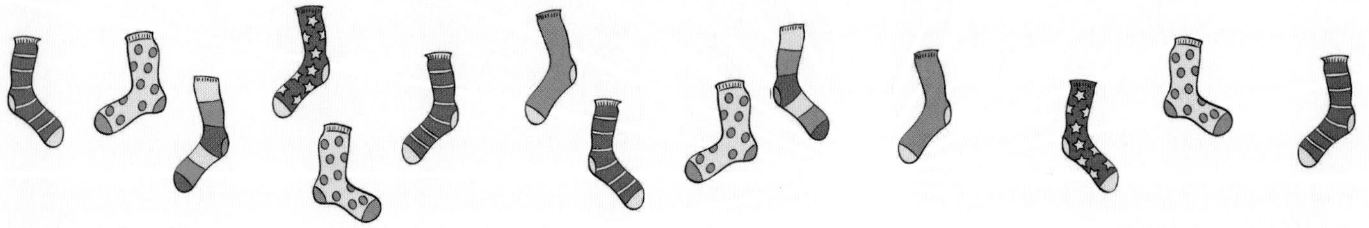

4 How many nests are there?

5 How many eggs altogether?

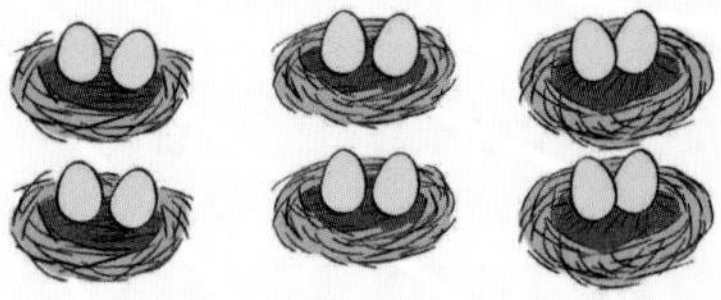

6 Colour the stars in twos.

5 x 2 =

7 How many pairs of boots are there?

8 How many boots are there altogether?

Now answer these questions.

9 3 x 2 =

10 1 x 2 =

11 6 x 2 =

12 2 x 2 =

13 7 x 2 =

14 4 x 2 =

Eight twos

My bike has two wheels.

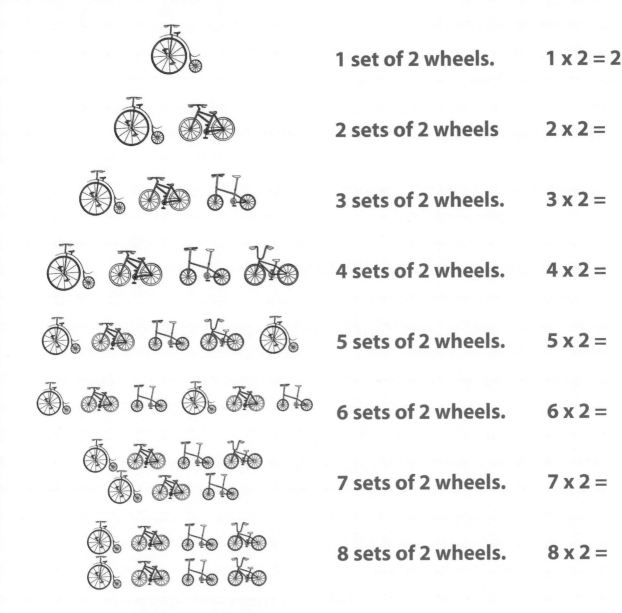

1 set of 2 wheels.	1 x 2 = 2
2 sets of 2 wheels	2 x 2 =
3 sets of 2 wheels.	3 x 2 =
4 sets of 2 wheels.	4 x 2 =
5 sets of 2 wheels.	5 x 2 =
6 sets of 2 wheels.	6 x 2 =
7 sets of 2 wheels.	7 x 2 =
8 sets of 2 wheels.	8 x 2 =

Look at this array of circles.

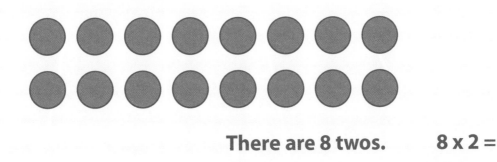

There are 8 twos.   8 x 2 =

Brodie's Brain Booster

How many wheels would nine bikes have altogether?

9

Nine twos

Flip-flops come in pairs too.

1 pair of trainers.   1 x 2 = 2

2 pairs of trainers.   2 x 2 =

3 pairs of trainers.   3 x 2 =

4 pairs of trainers.   4 x 2 =

5 pairs of trainers.   5 x 2 =

6 pairs of trainers.   6 x 2 =

7 pairs of trainers.   7 x 2 =

8 pairs of trainers.   8 x 2 =

9 pairs of trainers.   9 x 2 =

Look at these feet.

There are 9 pairs of feet.   9 x 2 =

Brodie's Brain Booster

How many feet would six children have altogether?

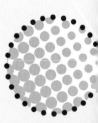

Ten times two

Look at the coins.

Ten 2p coins are worth 20p altogether.   10 x 2p =   p

Two 10p coins are also worth 20p altogether.   2 x 10p =   p

Colour the even numbers.

1 2 3 4 5 6 7 8 9 10
11 12 13 14 15 16 17 18 19 20

Which numbers did you colour?

11

Eleven twos

Eleven twos are twenty-two.

Look at this array of circles. Ring the circles in sets of two.
The first two sets have been done for you.

11 x 2 =

Complete the two times table up to 11 x 2.

one two is two	→	1 x 2 = 2
two twos are four	→	2 x 2 = 4
three twos are six	→	
four twos are eight	→	
five twos are ten	→	
six twos are twelve	→	
seven twos are fourteen	→	
eight twos are sixteen	→	
nine twos are eighteen	→	
ten twos are twenty	→	
eleven twos are twenty-two	→	

Brodie's
Brain Booster
I have eight 2p coins. How much money do I have altogether?

Twelve twos

Twelve twos are twenty-four.

Ring the blocks in sets of two. The first set has been done for you.

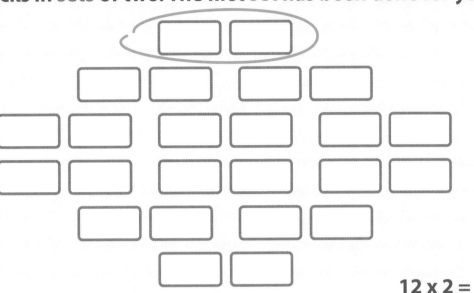

$$12 \times 2 =$$

This is the two times table.

one two is two	⟶	$1 \times 2 = 2$
two twos are four	⟶	$2 \times 2 = 4$
three twos are six	⟶	
four twos are eight	⟶	
five twos are ten	⟶	
six twos are twelve	⟶	
seven twos are fourteen	⟶	
eight twos are sixteen	⟶	
nine twos are eighteen	⟶	
ten twos are twenty	⟶	
eleven twos are twenty-two	⟶	
twelve twos are twenty-four	⟶	

1 **Write the missing numbers.**

1 ○ 3 ○ 5 ○ 7 ○ 9 ○ 11 ○

13 ○ 15 ○ 17 ○ 19 ○ 21 ○ 23 ○

2 **Ring the sets of two.**

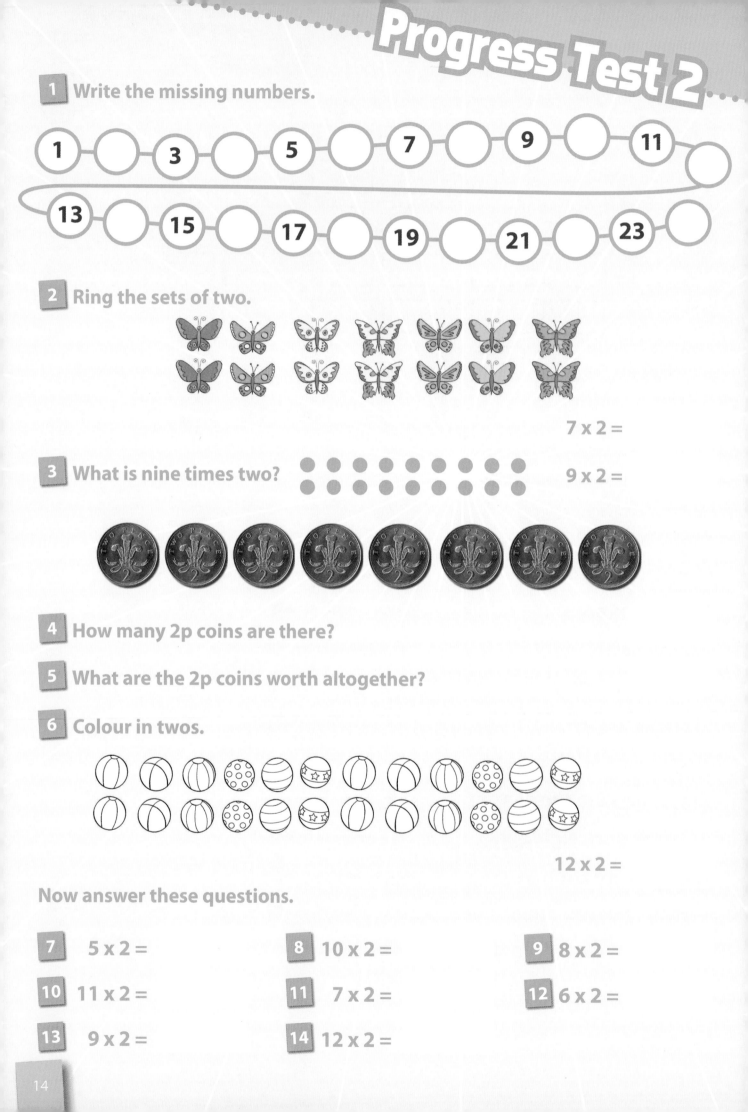

7 x 2 =

3 **What is nine times two?**

9 x 2 =

4 **How many 2p coins are there?**

5 **What are the 2p coins worth altogether?**

6 **Colour in twos.**

12 x 2 =

Now answer these questions.

7 5 x 2 =

8 10 x 2 =

9 8 x 2 =

10 11 x 2 =

11 7 x 2 =

12 6 x 2 =

13 9 x 2 =

14 12 x 2 =

14

Learning the five times table

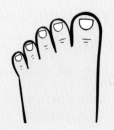

1 set of 5 toes,

so 5 toes altogether

1 x 5 = 5

3 sets of 5 toes,

so 15 toes altogether

5 + 5 + 5 = 15

3 x 5 =

2 sets of 5 toes,

so 10 toes altogether

5 + 5 = 10

2 x 5 = 10

4 sets of 5 toes,

so   toes altogether

5 + 5 + 5 + 5 =

4 x 5 =

Complete the first part of the five times table.

one five is five		1 x 5 =
two fives are ten		2 x 5 =
three fives are fifteen		
four fives are twenty		

Brodie's Brain Booster
I have three 5p coins. How much money do I have altogether?

Sets of five

Look at this array of circles. Ring the circles in sets of five. The first two sets have been done for you.

There are **5** sets of **5** circles.
There are **25** altogether. ———————➤ **5 x 5 = 25**

Ring the arrays in sets of five and fill in the answers.

3 x 5 =

2 x 5 =

4 x 5 =

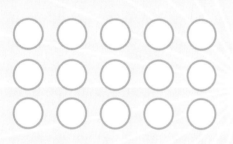

Brodie's Brain Booster

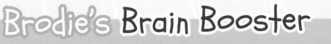
How many fingers would three people have altogether?

Did you know that two fives are the same as five twos?

Ring the circles in sets of two.

◯ ◯ ◯ ◯ ◯
◯ ◯ ◯ ◯ ◯

$5 \times 2 =$ ▢

Ring the circles in sets of five.

◯ ◯ ◯ ◯ ◯
◯ ◯ ◯ ◯ ◯

$2 \times 5 =$ ▢

Look at the coins, then fill in the answers.

$5 \times 2p =$ ▢

$2 \times 5p =$ ▢

Count in fives and colour the numbers you reach.

1 2 3 4 5 6 7 8 9 10
11 12 13 14 15 16 17 18 19 20
21 22 23 24 25 26 27 28 29 30

Which numbers did you colour?

▢ ▢ ▢ ▢ ▢ ▢

Six fives

Each monster has five eyes.

How many monsters are there?

How many eyes are there altogether?

Complete the first part of the five times table.

one five is five	➡	1 x 5 =
two fives are ten	➡	2 x 5 =
three fives are fifteen	➡	
four fives are twenty	➡	
five fives are twenty-five	➡	
six fives are thirty	➡	

Now answer these questions.

4 x 5 =	2 x 5 =	1 x 5 =
5 x 5 =	3 x 5 =	6 x 5 =

Brodie's Brain Booster

I have six 5p coins. How much money do I have altogether?

18

Seven fives

Can you find the five dots on a dice?

Count the dots on the dice.

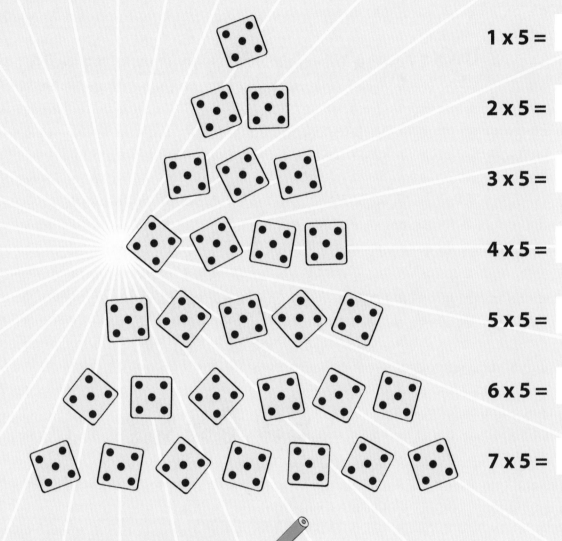

$1 \times 5 =$

$2 \times 5 =$

$3 \times 5 =$

$4 \times 5 =$

$5 \times 5 =$

$6 \times 5 =$

$7 \times 5 =$

Draw 8 dice each with 5 dots.

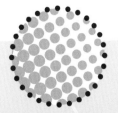

1 Write the missing numbers.

1 2 3 4 ◯ 6 7 8 9 ◯ 11 12

13 14 ◯ 16 17 18 19 ◯ 21 22 23 24 ◯

2 Colour in fives.

☆ ☆ ☆ ☆ ☆
☆ ☆ ☆ ☆ ☆
☆ ☆ ☆ ☆ ☆

3 x 5 =

3 How many gloves can you see?

4 How many glove fingers can you see?

5 How many 5p coins are there?

6 How much are the coins worth altogether?

7 How many dice are there?

8 How many dots are there altogether?

Now answer these questions.

9 3 x 5 =   **10** 1 x 5 =   **11** 6 x 5 =

12 2 x 5 =   **13** 5 x 5 =   **14** 4 x 5 =

Eight fives

A glove has five fingers.

1 x 5 = 5

2 x 5 =

3 x 5 =

4 x 5 =

5 x 5 =

6 x 5 =

7 x 5 =

8 x 5 =

Ring this array of dots in sets of 5.

There are 8 fives. 8 x 5 =

Brodie's Brain Booster

How many fingers would three children have altogether?

21

Nine fives

Most feet have five toes but mine don't!

1 foot has 5 toes.

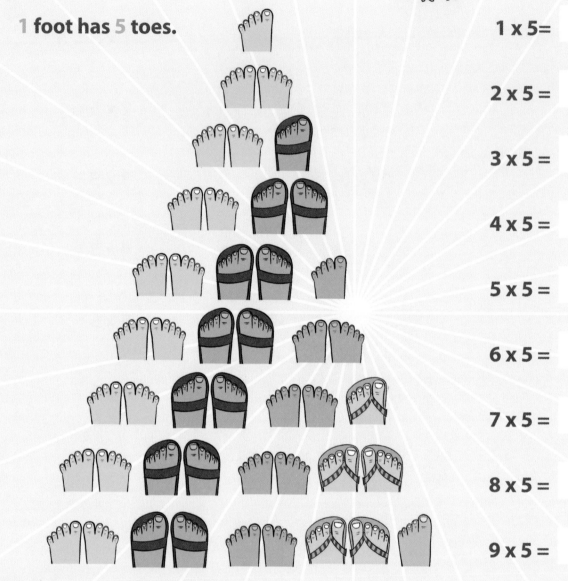

1 x 5=

2 x 5 =

3 x 5 =

4 x 5 =

5 x 5 =

6 x 5 =

7 x 5 =

8 x 5 =

9 x 5 =

Draw rings to make sets of 5.

How many sets of 5 are there?

How many are there altogether?

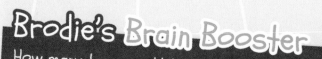

Brodie's Brain Booster
How many toes would ten feet have altogether?

Ten fives

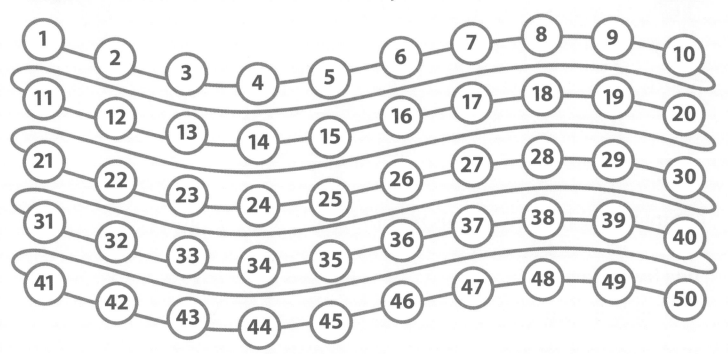

Ten fives are fifty.

Count in fives and colour the numbers you reach.

Which numbers did you colour?

Look at the coins.

Ten 5p coins are worth 50p altogether.   10 x 5p =   p

Five 10p coins are also worth 50p altogether.   5 x 10p =   p

Brodie's Brain Booster

I have six 5p coins. How much money do I have altogether?

Eleven fives

Look at this array of circles. Ring the circles in sets of five. The first two sets have been done for you.

$11 \times 5 =$

Complete the five times table up to 11 x 5.

one five is five	→	$1 \times 5 =$
two fives are ten	→	$2 \times 5 =$
three fives are fifteen	→	
four fives are twenty	→	
five fives are twenty-five	→	
six fives are thirty	→	
seven fives are thirty-five	→	
eight fives are forty	→	
nine fives are forty-five	→	
ten fives are fifty	→	
eleven fives are fifty-five	→	

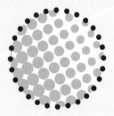

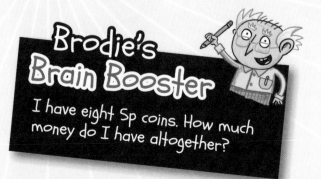

Brodie's Brain Booster

I have eight 5p coins. How much money do I have altogether?

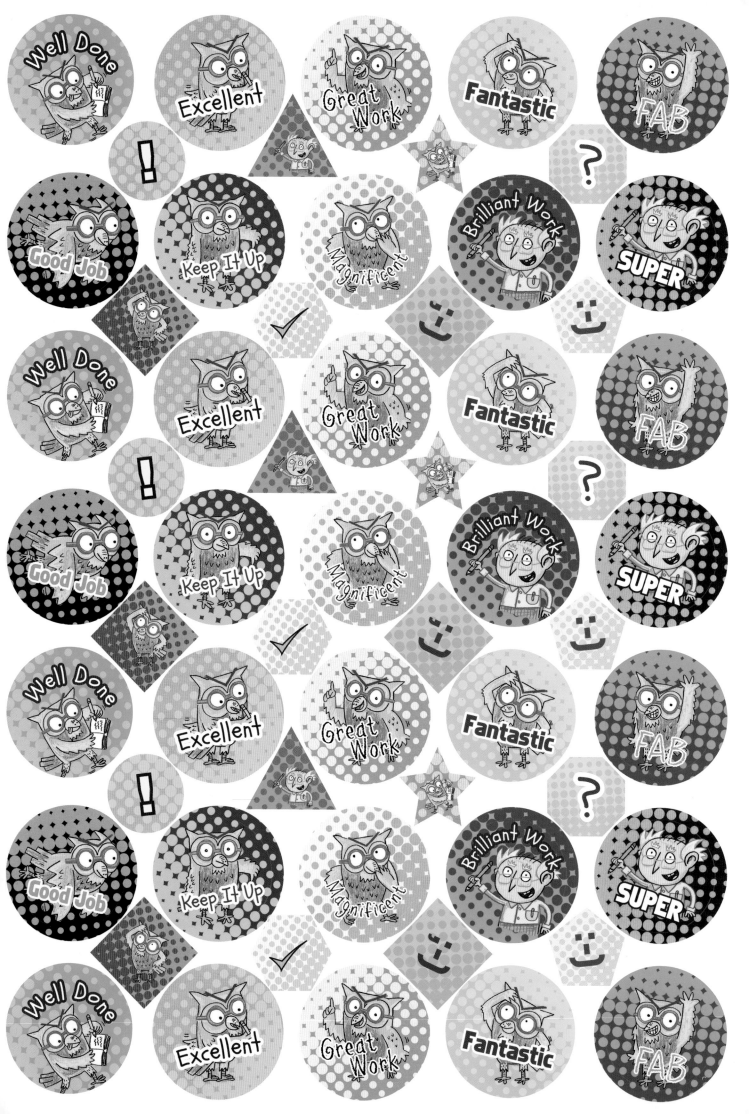

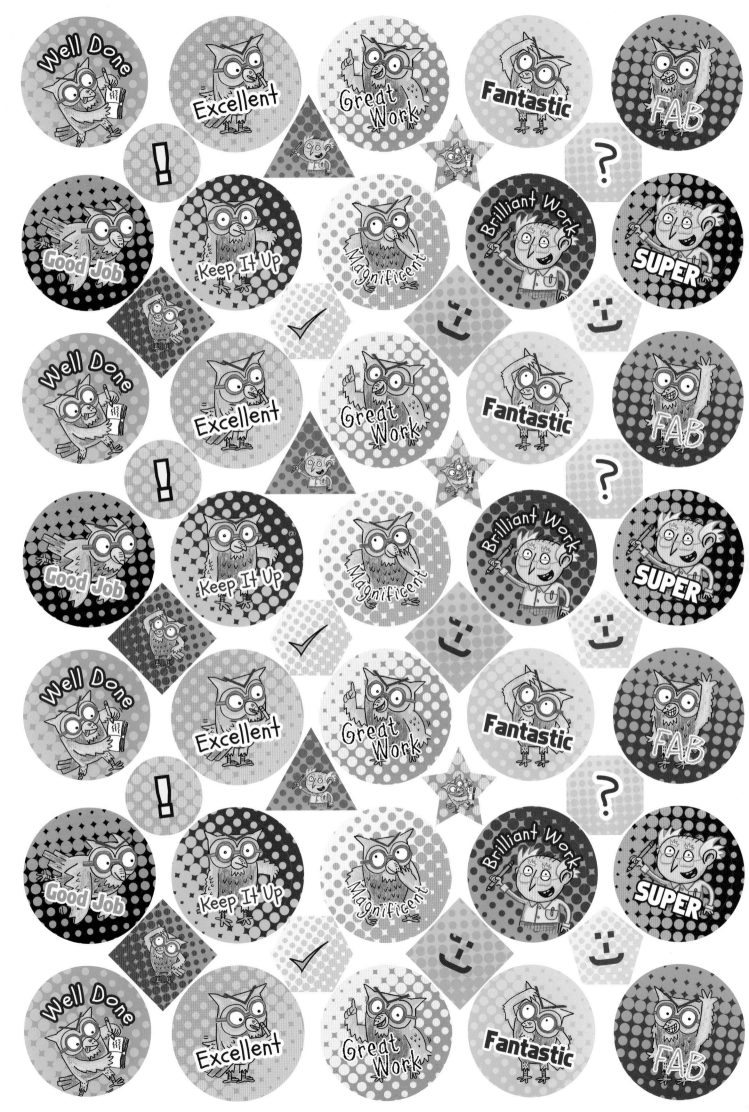

Twelve fives

Twelve fives are sixty.

sixty	thirty-five	twenty-five	forty-five	forty

thirty	fifteen	ten	twenty	fifty-five	five	fifty

Use the words above to fill in the five times table. Then complete the answers.

one five is	$\longrightarrow$	**1 x 5 =**
two fives are	$\longrightarrow$	**2 x 5 =**
three fives are	$\longrightarrow$	
four fives are	$\longrightarrow$	
five fives are	$\longrightarrow$	
six fives are	$\longrightarrow$	
seven fives are	$\longrightarrow$	
eight fives are	$\longrightarrow$	
nine fives are	$\longrightarrow$	
ten fives are	$\longrightarrow$	
eleven fives are	$\longrightarrow$	
twelve fives are	$\longrightarrow$	

25

1 Write the missing numbers.

1 — 2 — 3 — 4 — ◯ — 6 — 7 — 8 — 9 — ◯ — 11 — 12 — 13 — 14 — ◯ — 16 — 17

18 — 19 — ◯ — 21 — 22 — 23 — 24 — ◯ — 26 — 27 — 28 — 29 — ◯ — 31 — 32 — 33

34 — ◯ — 36 — 37 — 38 — 39 — ◯ — 41 — 42 — 43 — 44 — ◯ — 46 — 47 — 48 — 49 — ◯

2 Colour in fives.

4 x 5 =

3 What is nine times five?

4 How many 5p coins are there?

5 What are the 5p coins worth altogether?   p

6 Colour the dots.

12 x 5 =

Now answer these questions.

7 5 x 5 =

8 10 x 5 =

9 8 x 5 =

10 11 x 5 =

11 7 x 5 =

12 6 x 5 =

13 9 x 5 =

14 12 x 5 =

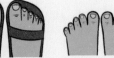

You've got ten toes altogether.

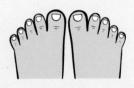

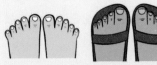

1 set of 10 toes,

so 10 toes altogether

1 x 10 = 10

3 sets of 10 toes,

so 30 toes altogether

10 + 10 + 10 = 30

3 x 10 =

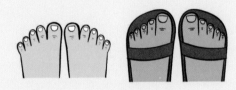

2 sets of 10 toes,

so 20 toes altogether

10 + 10 = 20

2 x 10 =

4 sets of 10 toes,

so ⬚ **toes altogether**

10 + 10 + 10 + 10 =

4 x 10 =

Complete the first part of the ten times table.

one ten is ten	⟶	1 x 10 =
two tens are twenty	⟶	2 x 10 =
three tens are thirty	⟶	3 x 10 =
four tens are forty	⟶	4 x 10 =

Brodie's Brain Booster

I have three 10p coins. How much money do I have altogether?

Five tens

Look at this **array** of circles. Ring the circles in sets of ten.
The first two sets have been done for you.

This array shows 5 sets of 10.
There are 50 circles altogether. ➜ **5 x 10 = 50**

Colour the arrays in sets of ten.

3 x 10 =

4 x 10 =

2 x 10 =

Brodie's Brain Booster
How many fingers would six children have altogether?

Ring the circles in sets of two.

○○○○○○○○○○
○○○○○○○○○○

10 x 2 =

Ring the circles in sets of ten.

○○○○○○○○○○
○○○○○○○○○○

2 x 10 =

Look at the coins, then fill in the answers.

10 x 2p = ☐ p

2 x 10p = ☐ p

Colour the numbers in the ten times table.

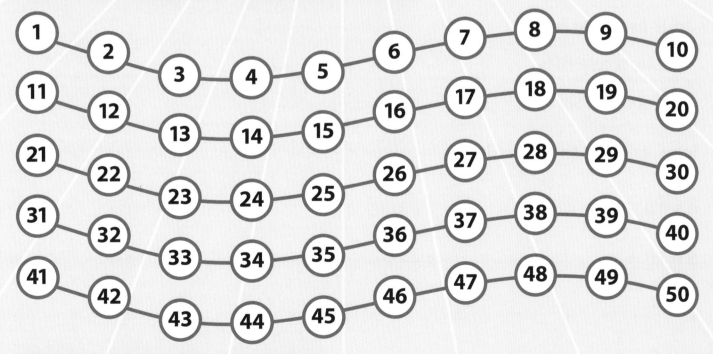

Which numbers did you colour?

☐ ☐ ☐ ☐

Six tens

Each creature has ten legs.

How many creatures are there?

How many legs are there altogether?

Complete the first part of the ten times table.

one ten is ten	→	**1 x 10 =**
two tens are twenty	→	**2 x 10 =**
three tens are thirty	→	
four tens are forty	→	
five tens are fifty	→	
six tens are sixty	→	

Now answer the questions.

4 x 10 =   2 x 10 =   1 x 10 =

5 x 10 =   3 x 10 =   6 x 10 =

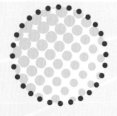

Brodie's Brain Booster

I have six 10p coins. How much money do I have altogether?

30

Seven tens

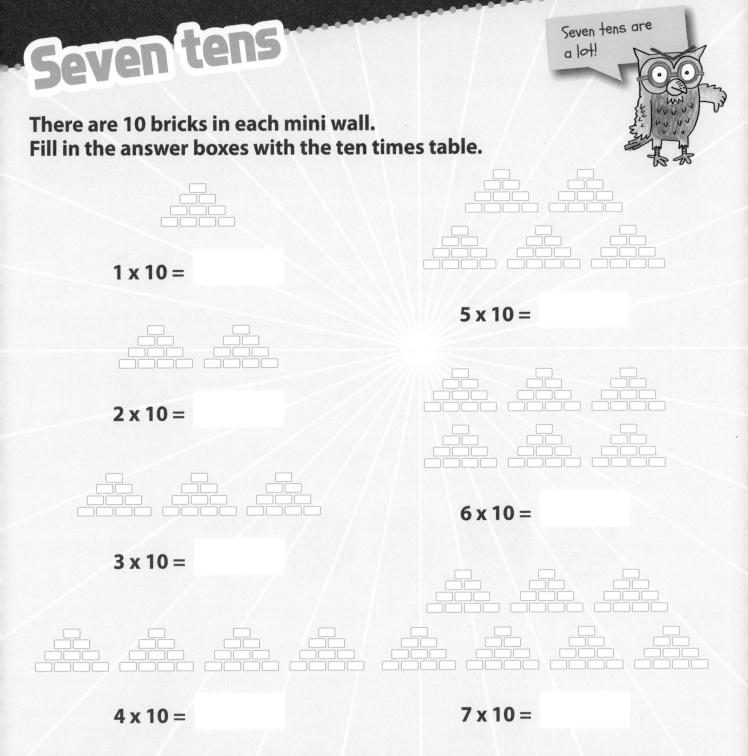

Seven tens are a lot!

There are 10 bricks in each mini wall.
Fill in the answer boxes with the ten times table.

1 x 10 =

2 x 10 =

3 x 10 =

4 x 10 =

5 x 10 =

6 x 10 =

7 x 10 =

Draw 8 mini walls each with 10 bricks then write the times table it shows.

31

1 Write the missing numbers.

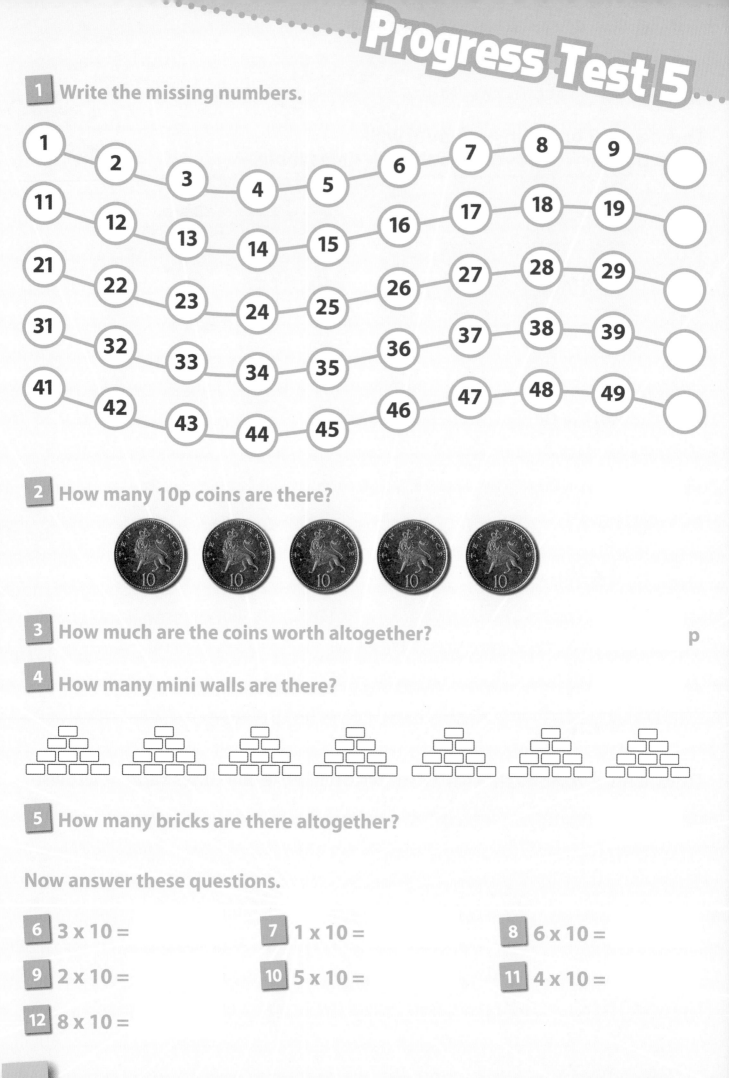

2 How many 10p coins are there?

3 How much are the coins worth altogether?   p

4 How many mini walls are there?

5 How many bricks are there altogether?

Now answer these questions.

6 3 x 10 =   **7** 1 x 10 =   **8** 6 x 10 =

9 2 x 10 =   **10** 5 x 10 =   **11** 4 x 10 =

12 8 x 10 =

Eight tens

I'm glad I've only got two legs.

1 set of 10 legs.   1 x 10 = 10

2 sets of 10 legs.   2 x 10 =

3 sets of 10 legs.   3 x 10 =

4 sets of 10 legs.   4 x 10 =

5 sets of 10 legs.   5 x 10 =

6 sets of 10 legs.   6 x 10 =

7 sets of 10 legs.   7 x 10 =

8 sets of 10 legs.   8 x 10 =

Now see if you can answer these questions.

10 + 10 =

10 + 10 + 10 =

10 + 10 +10 +10 =

10 + 10 +10 +10 +10 =

10 + 10 +10 +10 +10 + 10 =

10 + 10 +10 +10 +10 +10 +10 =

10 + 10 +10 +10 +10 +10 +10 +10 =

Brodie's Brain Booster

How many fingers would eight children have altogether?

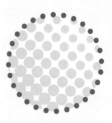

Nine tens

Each creature has ten legs.

How many creatures are there?

How many legs are there altogether?

Complete this part of the ten times table.

one ten is ten	⟶	1 x 10 =
two tens are twenty	⟶	2 x 10 =
three tens are thirty	⟶	
four tens are forty	⟶	
five tens are fifty	⟶	
six tens are sixty	⟶	
seven tens are seventy	⟶	
eight tens are eighty	⟶	
nine tens are ninety	⟶	

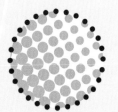

Brodie's Brain Booster

I have nine 10p coins. How much money do I have altogether?

Ten times ten

Ten tens are one hundred.

Count in tens and colour the numbers you reach.

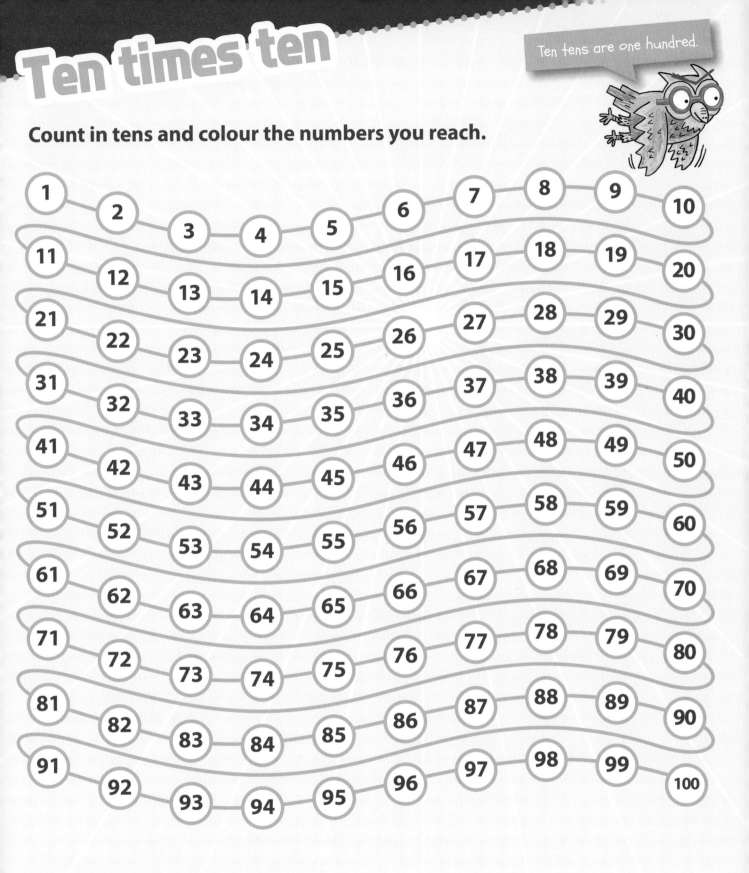

1 2 3 4 5 6 7 8 9 10
11 12 13 14 15 16 17 18 19 20
21 22 23 24 25 26 27 28 29 30
31 32 33 34 35 36 37 38 39 40
41 42 43 44 45 46 47 48 49 50
51 52 53 54 55 56 57 58 59 60
61 62 63 64 65 66 67 68 69 70
71 72 73 74 75 76 77 78 79 80
81 82 83 84 85 86 87 88 89 90
91 92 93 94 95 96 97 98 99 100

Which numbers did you colour?

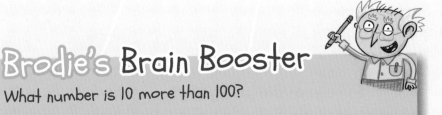

Brodie's Brain Booster

What number is 10 more than 100?

35

Eleven tens

Eleven tens are a hundred and ten.

Look at this array of circles. Ring the circles in sets of ten. The first two sets have been done for you.

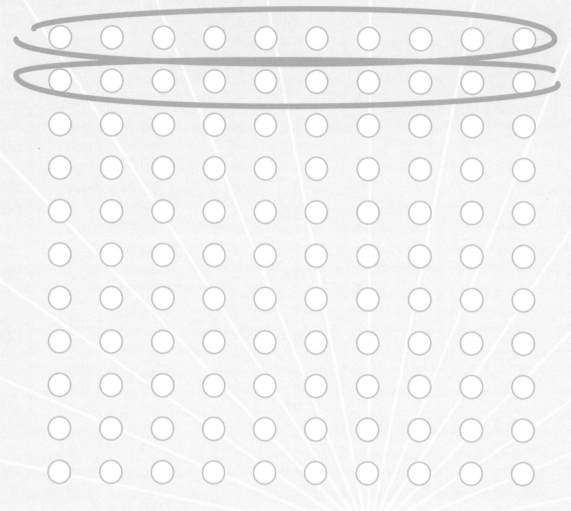

11 x 10 =

Now answer the questions.

6 x 10 =   3 x 10 =   9 x 10 =

4 x 10 =   10 x 10 =   7 x 10 =

2 x 10 =   8 x 10 =   5 x 10 =

1 x 10 =   11 x 10 =

Brodie's Brain Booster

I have eight 10p coins. How much money do I have altogether?

36

Twelve tens

Twelve tens are one hundred and twenty.

Ring in sets of 10. The first one has been done for you.

$$12 \times 10 =$$

Brodie's Brain Booster

How many fingers would eight children have altogether?

1 Write the missing numbers.

10   20   30   50   70   90   100

2 Colour in tens.

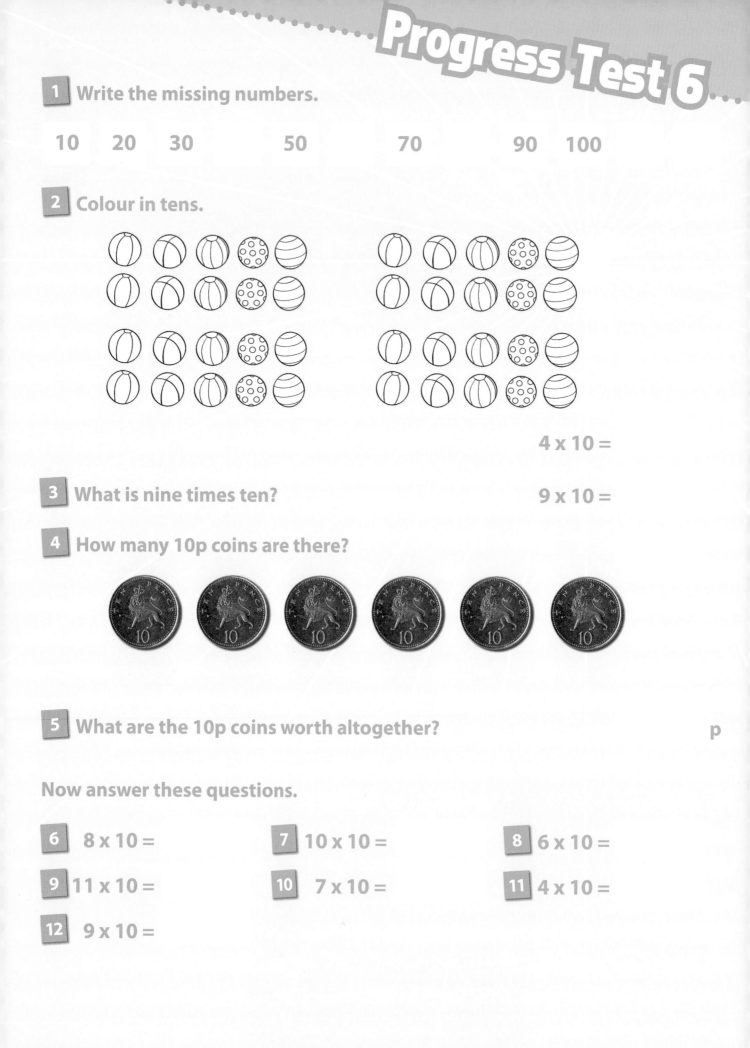

4 x 10 =

3 What is nine times ten?   9 x 10 =

4 How many 10p coins are there?

5 What are the 10p coins worth altogether?   p

Now answer these questions.

6 8 x 10 =   **7** 10 x 10 =   **8** 6 x 10 =

9 11 x 10 =   **10** 7 x 10 =   **11** 4 x 10 =

12 9 x 10 =

Two times table

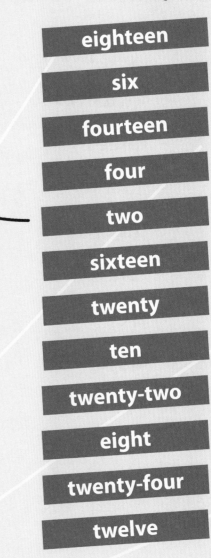

Draw lines to join the two times table together.

one two	eighteen
two twos	six
three twos	fourteen
four twos	four
five twos	two
six twos	sixteen
seven twos	twenty
eight twos	ten
nine twos	twenty-two
ten twos	eight
eleven twos	twenty-four
twelve twos	twelve

Now write the two times table.

1 x 2 = 2

Brodie's Brain Booster

How many feet would eight owls have altogether?

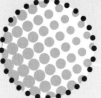

Five times table

Do you remember the five times table?

Draw lines to join the five times table together.

one five	twenty
two fives	fifteen
three fives	forty
four fives	forty-five
five fives	thirty-five
six fives	five
seven fives	ten
eight fives	fifty
nine fives	sixty
ten fives	twenty-five
eleven fives	thirty
twelve fives	fifty-five

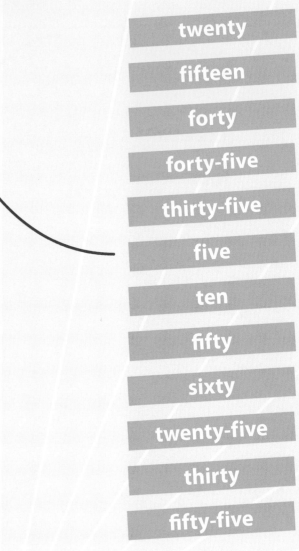

Now write the five times table.

1 x 5 = 5

Brodie's Brain Booster

How many fingers would seven hands have altogether?

Ten times table check

Draw lines to join the ten times table together.

one ten	thirty
two tens	ninety
three tens	sixty
four tens	twenty
five tens	ten
six tens	seventy
seven tens	one hundred and ten
eight tens	fifty
nine tens	forty
ten tens	one hundred and twenty
eleven tens	one hundred
twelve tens	eighty

Now write the ten times table.

1 x 10 = 10	

Brodie's Brain Booster

How many fingers would five people have altogether?

How much money can you see in each piggy bank?
The first one has been done for you.

30p

I like coins when they are shiny.

2p   5p   10p   20p   50p

Here is 10p. Draw 2p coins that are worth the same.

Draw 5p coins that are worth the same as 10p.

Here is 50p. Draw 10p coins that are worth the same as 50p.

Here is 20p. Draw 5p coins that are worth the same as 20p.

1 Write the missing numbers.

| 10 | | 30 | | | 60 | | | 90 | |

2 How much money is in the piggy bank?   p

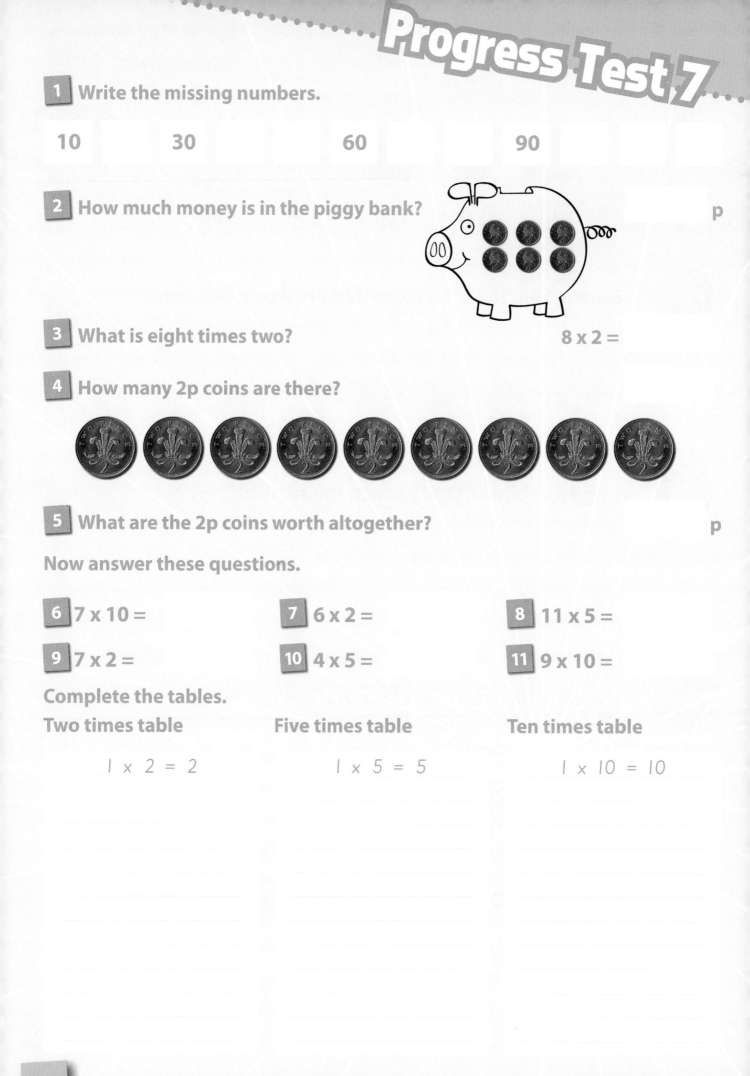

3 What is eight times two?   8 x 2 =

4 How many 2p coins are there?

5 What are the 2p coins worth altogether?   p

Now answer these questions.

6 7 x 10 =   **7** 6 x 2 =   **8** 11 x 5 =

9 7 x 2 =   **10** 4 x 5 =   **11** 9 x 10 =

Complete the tables.

Two times table	Five times table	Ten times table
I x 2 = 2	I x 5 = 5	I x 10 = 10

ANSWERS

Page 3

4 sets of 2 eyes: 8, 8, 8

3 sets of 2 eyes: 6

5 sets of 2 eyes: 10, 10, 10

3×2=6, 4×2=8, 5×2=10

Page 4

Check that your child has circled the remaining 3 sets of 2.

Check that your child has circled 3 sets of 2. 3×2=6

Check that your child has circled 1 set of 2. 1×2=2

Check that your child has circled 4 sets of 2. 4×2=8

Check that your child has circled 2 sets of 2. 2×2=4

Brain Booster: 6

Page 5

Check that your child has joined the matching pairs.

2×2=4, 3×2=6, 4×2=8, 5×2=10

Check that your child has coloured 2, 4, 6, 8 and 10.

Page 6

6 pairs of boots

12 boots altogether

6×2=12

Check that your child has joined the matching pairs. 6×2=12

3×2=6, 4×2=8, 5×2=10, 6×2=12

Check that your child has coloured 2, 4, 6, 8, 10 and 12.

Brain Booster: 14

Page 7

7 nests

14 eggs

7×2=14

Check that your child has circled 7 sets of 2. 7×2=14

3×2=6, 4×2=8, 5×2=10, 6×2=12, 7×2=14

Check that your child has coloured 2, 4, 6, 8, 10, 12 and 14.

Page 8 • Progress Test 1

1. Missing numbers: 2, 4, 6, 8, 10, 12, 14
2. Check that your child has circled 4 sets of 2. 4×2=8
3. Check that your child has joined the matching pairs. 7x2=14
4. 6 nests
5. 12 eggs
6. Check that your child has coloured 5 sets of 2. 5×2=10
7. 3 pairs of boots
8. 6 boots altogether
9. 3×2=6
10. 1×2=2
11. 6×2=12
12. 2×2=4
13. 7×2=14
14. 4×2=8

Page 9

2×2=4

3×2=6

4×2=8

5×2=10

6×2=12

7×2=14

8×2=16

8×2=16

Brain Booster: 18 wheels

Page 10

2×2=4

3×2=6

4×2=8

5×2=10

6×2=12

7×2=14

8×2=16

9×2=18

9×2=18

Brain Booster: 12 feet

Page 11

10×2p=20p

2×10p=20p

Check that your child has coloured 2, 4, 6, 8, 10, 12, 14, 16, 18 and 20.

Page 12

Check that your child has circled 11 sets of 2. 11×2=22

3×2=6

4×2=8

5×2=10

6×2=12

7×2=14

8×2=16

9×2=18

10×2=20

11×2=22

Brain Booster: 16p

Page 13

Check that your child has circled 12 sets of 2. 12×2=24

3×2=6

4×2=8

5×2=10

6×2=12

7×2=14

8×2=16

9×2=18

10×2=20

11×2=22

12×2=24

Page 14 • Progress Test 2

1. Missing numbers: 2,4,6,8,10,12,14,16,18,20,22,24
2. Check that your child has circled 7 sets of 2. 7×2=14
3. 9×2=18
4. 8
5. 16p
6. Check that your child has coloured 12 sets of 2. 12×2=24
7. 5×2=10
8. 10×2=20
9. 8×2=16
10. 11×2=22
11. 7×2=14
12. 6×2=12
13. 9×2=18
14. 12×2=24

Page 15

3 sets of 5 toes: 15

4 sets of 5 toes: 20, 20, 20

1×5=5

2×5=10

3×5=15

4×5=20

Brain Booster: 15p

Page 16

Check that your child has circled the remaining 3 sets of 5.

Check that your child has circled 3 sets of 5. 3×5=15

Check that your child has circled 2 sets of 5. 2×5=10

Check that your child has circled 4 sets of 5. 4×5=20

Brain Booster: 30 fingers

Page 17

Check that your child has circled 5 sets of 2. 5×2=10

Check that your child has circled 2 sets of 5. 2×5=10

5×2p=10p

2×5p=10p

Check that your child has coloured 5, 10, 15, 20, 25 and 30.

Page 18

6 monsters

30 eyes

1×5=5

2×5=10

3×5=15

4×5=20

5×5=25

6×5=30

4×5=20, 2×5=10, 1×5=5

5×5=25, 3×5=15, 6×5=30

Brain Booster: 30p

Page 19

1×5=5

2×5=10

3×5=15

4×5=20

5×5=25

6×5=30

7×5=35

Check that your child has drawn 8 dice with 5 dots each.

Page 20 • Progress Test 3

1. Missing numbers: 5, 10, 15, 20, 25
2. Check that your child has coloured 3 sets of 5. 3×5=15
3. 8 gloves
4. 40 glove fingers
5. 3 coins
6. 15p
7. 7 dice
8. 35 dots
9. 3×5=15
10. 1×5=5
11. 6×5=30
12. 2×5=10
13. 5×5=25
14. 4×5=20

Page 21

2×5=10

3×5=15

4×5=20

5×5=25

6×5=30

7×5=35

8×5=40

Check that your child has circled 8 sets of 5. 8×5=40

Brain Booster: 30 fingers

Page 22

1×5=5

2×5=10

3×5=15

4×5=20

5×5=25

6×5=30

7×5=35

8×5=40

9×5=45

Check that your child has circled 5 sets of 5

25 stars altogether

Brain Booster: 50 toes

Page 23

Check that your child has coloured 5, 10, 15, 20, 25, 30, 35, 40, 45 and 50

10×5p=50p

5×10p=50p

Brain Booster: 30p

Page 24

Check that your child has circled the remaining 9 sets of 5. 11×5=55

1×5=5

2×5=10

3×5=15

4×5=20

5×5=25

6×5=30

7×5=35

8×5=40

9×5=45

10×5=50

11×5=55

Brain Booster: 40p

Page 25

one five is five	1×5=5
two fives are ten	2×5=10
three fives are fifteen	3×5=15
four fives are twenty	4×5=20
five fives are twenty-five	5×5=25
six fives are thirty	6×5=30
seven fives are thirty-five	7×5=35
eight fives are forty	8×5=40
nine fives are forty-five	9×5=45
ten fives are fifty	10×5=50
eleven fives are fifty five	11×5=55
twelve fives are sixty	12×5=60

Page 26 • Progress Test 4

1. Missing numbers: 5, 10, 15, 20, 25, 30, 35, 40, 45, 50
2. Check that your child has coloured 4 sets of 5. 4×5=20
3. 9×5=45
4. 7 coins
5. 35p
6. Check that your child has coloured 12 sets of 5 dots. 12×5=60
7. 5×5=25
8. 10×5=50
9. 8×5=40
10. 11×5=55
11. 7×5=35
12. 6×5=30
13. 9×5=45
14. 12×5=60

Page 27

3 sets of 10 toes: 30

2 sets of 10 toes: 20

4 sets of 10 toes: 40, 40, 40

1×10=10

2×10=20

3×10=30

4×10=40

Brain Booster: 30p

Page 28

Check that your child has circled the remaining 3 sets of 10.

Check that your child has circled 3 sets of 10. 3×10=30

Check that your child has circled 4 sets of 10. 4×10=40

Check that your child has circled 2 sets of 10. 2×10=20

Brain Booster: 60 fingers

Page 29

Check that your child has circled 10 sets of 2. 10×2=20

Check that your child has circled 2 sets of 10. 2×10=20

20p

20p

Check that your child has coloured 10, 20, 30, 40 and 50

Page 30

6 creatures

60 legs altogether

1×10=10

2×10=20

3×10=30

4×10=40

5×10=50

6×10=60

4×10=40, 2×10=20, 1×10=10

5×10=50, 3×10=30, 6×10=60

Brain Booster: 60p

Page 31

1×10=10

5×10=50

2×10=20

6×10=60

3×10=30

4×10=40

7×10=70

Check that your child has drawn 8 walls with 10 bricks in each. 8×10=80

Page 32 • Progress Test 5

1. Missing numbers: 10, 20, 30, 40, 50
2. 5 coins
3. 50p
4. 7 walls
5. 70 bricks
6. 3×10=30
7. 1×10=10
8. 6×10=60
9. 2×10=20
10. 5×10=50
11. 4×10=40
12. 8×10=80

Page 33

2×10=20

3×10=30

4×10=40

5×10=50

6×10=60

7×10=70

8×10=80

10+10=20

10+10+10=30

10+10+10+10=40

10+10+10+10+10=50

10+10+10+10+10+10=60

10+10+10+10+10+10+10=70

10+10+10+10+10+10+10+10=80

Brain Booster: 80 fingers

Page 34

9 creatures

90 legs altogether

1×10=10

2×10=20

3×10=30

4×10=40

5×10=50

6×10=60

7×10=70

8×10=80

9×10=90

Brain Booster: 90p

Page 35

Check that your child has coloured 10, 20, 30, 40, 50, 60, 70, 80, 90 and 100

Brain Booster: 110

Page 36

Check that your child has coloured the remaining 9 sets of 10. 11×10=110

6×10=60, 3×10=30, 9×10=90

4×10=40, 10×10=100, 7×10=70

2×10=20, 8×10=80, 5×10=50

1×10=10, 11×10=110

Brain Booster: 80p

Page 37

Check that your child has circled the remaining 11 sets of 10. 12×10=120

Brain Booster: 80

Page 38 • Progress Test 6

1. Missing numbers: 40, 60, 80, 110, 120
2. Check that your child has coloured 4 sets of 10. 4×10=40
3. 9×10=90
4. 6 coins
5. 60p
6. 8×10=80
7. 10×10=100
8. 6×10=60
9. 11×10=110
10. 7×10=70
11. 4×10=40
12. 9×10=90

Page 39

Check that your child has drawn lines to match the boxes

one two – two

two twos – four

three twos – six

four twos – eight

five twos – ten

six twos – twelve

seven twos – fourteen

eight twos – sixteen

nine twos – eighteen

ten twos – twenty

eleven twos – twenty-two

twelve twos – twenty-four

1×2=2

2×2=4

3×2=6

4×2=8

5×2=10

6×2=12
7×2=14
8×2=16
9×2=18
10×2=20
11×2=22
12×2=24

Brain Booster: 16 feet

Page 40

Check that your child has drawn lines to match the boxes

one five – five

two fives – ten

three fives – fifteen

four fives – twenty

five fives – twenty-five

six fives – thirty

seven fives – thirty-five

eight fives – forty

nine fives – forty-five

ten fives – fifty

eleven fives – fifty-five

twelve fives – sixty

1×5=5
2×5=10
3×5=15
4×5=20
5×5=25
6×5=30
7×5=35
8×5=40
9×5=45
10×5=50
11×5=55
12×5=60

Brain Booster: 35 fingers

Page 41

Check that your child has drawn lines to match the boxes

one ten – ten

two tens – twenty

three tens – thirty

four tens – forty

five tens – fifty

six tens – sixty

seven tens – seventy

eight tens – eighty

nine tens – ninety

ten tens – one hundred

eleven tens – one hundred and ten

twelve tens – one hundred and twenty

1×10=10
2×10=20
3×10=30
4×10=40
5×10=50
6×10=60
7×10=70
8×10=80
9×10=90
10×10=100
11×10=110
12×10=120

Brain Booster: 50 fingers

Page 42

80p

10p, 14p

60p, 25p

40p, 20p

40p

Page 43

Check that your child has drawn five 2p coins.

Check that your child has drawn two 5p coins.

Check that you child has drawn five 10p coins.

Check that your child has drawn four 5p coins.

Page 44 • Progress Test 7

1. Missing numbers: 20, 40, 50, 70, 80, 100, 110, 120
2. 60p
3. 8×2=16
4. 9 coins
5. 18p
6. 7×10=70
7. 6×2=12
8. 11×5=55
9. 7×2=14
10. 4×5=20
11. 9×10=90

1x2=2
2x2=4
3x2=6
4×2=8
5×2=10
6×2=12
7×2=14
8×2=16
9×2=18
10×2=20
11×2=22
12×2=24

1×5=5
2×5=10
3×5=15
4×5=20
5×5=25
6×5=30
7×5=35
8×5=40
9×5=45
10×5=50
11×5=55
12×5=60

1×10=10
2×10=20
3×10=30
4×10=40
5×10=50
6×10=60
7×10=70
8×10=80
9×10=90
10×10=100
11×10=110
12×10=120